**W9-DBZ-829**

One Direction
Popular Boy Band

by Lucas Diver

ABDO
POP BIOS
Kids

abdopublishing.com

Published by Abdo Kids, a division of ABDO, PO Box 398166, Minneapolis, Minnesota 55439.

Copyright © 2015 by Abdo Consulting Group, Inc. International copyrights reserved in all countries. No part of this book may be reproduced in any form without written permission from the publisher.

Printed in the United States of America, North Mankato, Minnesota.

102014

012015

THIS BOOK CONTAINS
RECYCLED MATERIALS

Photo Credits: AP Images, iStock, Shutterstock,
© JStone p5,17,21 © Featureflash p13 © Andrea Raffin p15 / Shutterstock

Production Contributors: Teddy Borth, Jennie Forsberg, Grace Hansen

Design Contributors: Laura Rask, Dorothy Toth

Library of Congress Control Number: 2014943780

Cataloging-in-Publication Data

Diver, Lucas.

One Direction: popular boy band / Lucas Diver.

p. cm. -- (Pop bios)

Includes index.

ISBN 978-1-62970-726-6

1. One Direction (Musical group)--Biography--Juvenile literature. 2. Rock musicians --England--
Biography--Juvenile literature. 3. Boy bands--England--Juvenile literature. 1. Title.

782.42164092/2--dc23

[B]

2014943780

Table of Contents

1D

One Direction (1D) is a pop boy band. There are five members. Their names are Niall, Liam, Harry, Louis, and Zayn.

4

The X Factor

In 2010, each boy tried

out for The X Factor.

None of them made it **solo**.

The judges had an idea.
The boys would form a
band. They would perform
on the show together.

They were very **popular** on the show. They won third place!

11

Up All Night

1D signed with a **label**.
They released their first
album. Their first **single** was
"What Makes You Beautiful."

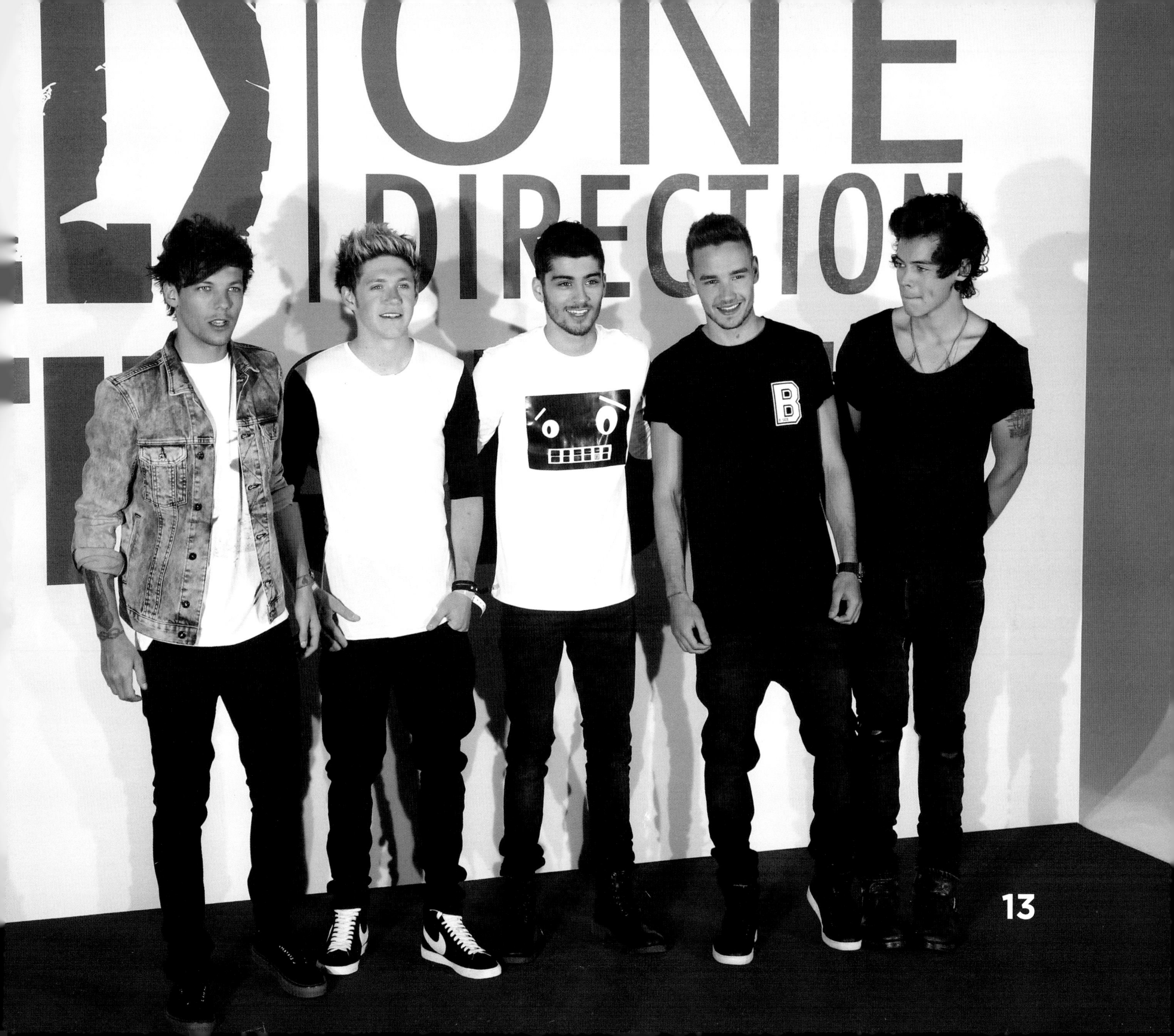
ONE
DIRECTION

The album hit number

one in the United States.

It was number one in

15 other countries too.

1D was a huge **success**.
They were given another
record deal. This one
was in the United States.

17

Two More Albums

1D released their second
album in November 2012.
Their third album came
out in November 2013.

19

Fans from around

the world love 1D.

Timeline

September
1D's first single, "What Makes You Beautiful" is released. It is a huge hit.

December
One Direction places third on X Factor.

November
1D's third album, *Midnight Memories* is released.

2010

2011

2013

2010

2011

2012

2014

July
Each boy is sent home from X Factor. All are brought back to perform as a group.

January
Simon Cowell signs 1D to a record deal. Their first album, *Up All Night* is released.

November
1D's second album, *Take Me Home* is released.

February
1D's World Tour begins.

Glossary

label – short for record label. A company that produces, creates, distributes, and markets the album, and more.

popular – well-known and liked by many people.

single – a song released separately from an album. The song is popular and promotes the album.

solo – to perform as a single person and not in a band.

success – achieve fame.

Index

abdokids.com

Use this code to log on to abdokids.com and access crafts, games, videos, and more!

Abdo Kids Code:
POK7266